THE BROCKHA...

C000146705

guide
Tarot
Cards

BROCKHAMPTON PRESS
LONDON

This edition published 1996 by Brockhampton Press,
a member of Hodder Headline PLC Group.

ISBN 1 86019 287 4

Printed and bound in the UK

Contents

Introduction

The Tarot pack is a set of illustrated cards which may be used for predicting future events or for answering almost any kind of question put to it through someone familiar with its symbolism. As a divination technique, it offers possibilities not contained in any other system and it is the only predictive method that is possible for anyone to understand and use after only a few weeks of study and practice. As with all arts, only years of experience will bring full proficiency, but mastering the Tarot does not require the unleashing of dark, supernatural forces or the invoking of ghostly spirits, as many would think, but rather requires an openness to impressions coming from the unconscious mind. We all have this ability—it manifests itself in precognitive dreams, feelings of foreboding, good or bad impressions of people we meet—but we usually ignore these feelings, dismissing them as irrational. Tarot reading is a way of harnessing these intuitive feelings and using them for personal guidance.

History of the Tarot

There is little agreement on when and where the Tarot originated. The earliest cards used in Europe bear some similarity to cards used much earlier in Egypt, India and China, but there is little evidence of a direct link. One theory suggests that gypsies brought the cards with them from the east, but while it is true that travelling people have used them for centuries in fortune-telling, it is unlikely that they invented them. Another theory is that the cards are named after the River Taro in the north of Italy and that the cards were invented in the area around there.

For many centuries cards similar in design to those in use today could be found in wealthy European households. These cards were more likely to be for playing games than for purposes of divination, and their popularity rose and fell depending on the fashion of the day. When they were in vogue, draughtsmen and printers, unfamiliar with the Tarot, would rush out new sets of cards to satisfy demand. This inevitably led to the designs being altered as each new set had some small detail added or left out.

It was not until the eighteenth century that people started taking the Tarot more seriously. This was the Age of Enlightenment and there was a great deal of interest in the customs, religious beliefs and ideas of ancient civilizations. Antoine Court de Gébelin, an archaeologist and amateur occult scholar from the south of France, wrote a series of books on a diverse range of esoteric subjects and claimed that the Tarot had its origins in an ancient Egyptian text called *The Book of Thoth*. That de Gébelin's theories were so readily accepted can be attributed to the widespread passion for 'Egyptiana' at the time in European society. Hieroglyphic writing, years before the discovery of the Rosetta Stone, frustrated antiquarians, and it became fashionable to suggest that the apparently indecipherable symbols could provide answers to questions that had plagued mankind since the earliest times. De Gébelin followed this trend and made a connection between the Tarot and Egypt, which was popular but which had no basis in fact.

Nevertheless, many writers took up de Gébelin's theories and attempted to expand on them. But when the hieroglyphics were finally deciphered and it was discovered that there was little or no connection between them and the Tarot, those seeking a mystic source had to look elsewhere. Alphonse Louis Constant, writing as Eliphas Lévi, eventually came up with a connection to ancient Hebrew beliefs in two books published in 1855 and 1856. This featured the Jewish mystical system of the Cabbala, which linked letters of the Hebrew alphabet to numbers. He devised a new system of Tarot, which more correctly reflected his theories, but again no hard evidence was offered as to the origins of the cards.

Today we do not know much more than in de Gébelin or Lévi's time. There has been a great deal of speculation and many claims for the source of the Tarot—other writers have linked it with Sufi and Cabbalistic origins or found connections with Greek mythology and pre-Christian religions—but so little evidence to substantiate any claim has been forthcoming that it would appear that the true origins of the Tarot are forever going to remain a mystery.

Reading the Cards

The Tarot pack most commonly used today is based on an Italian form known as the Venetian or Piedmontese Tarot which became the standard version in that country by the beginning of the sixteenth century. There are 78 cards in this pack, divided into two parts: the Major Arcana (22 cards) and the Minor Arcana (56 cards). 'Arcana' means secrets or mysteries.

The Major Arcana cards, also known as the Trump cards, display mysterious, esoteric imagery which seems to be influenced by pagan traditions. From pack to pack there may be differences in style, position of the figure, dress and other details, but there is a strong common symbolism and their interpretation remains more or less constant. The Minor Arcana features 56 cards divided into four suits, each suit having ten Pip cards and four Court cards. This is a similar arrangement to a normal pack of playing cards, except for the Knight cards in each suit. The Tarot suits correspond to playing card suits but have different names: Wands (also known as Batons or Rods) correspond to Clubs; Cups correspond to Hearts; Swords to Spades and Pentacles (also known as Coins or Discs) to Diamonds.

Selecting your Cards

Before one can embark on a reading of the Tarot it is important that you are happy with the cards that you intend to use. Tarot convention decrees that effective readings can only be obtained if the reader uses cards which they feel comfortable and familiar with—using someone else's cards, therefore, is seriously frowned upon. This is because everyone has a different psychic energy and cards owned and used by one person will have a unique psychic identity impressed on them. Cards should also be wrapped in a piece of silk and kept in a wooden box when not in use. Again, this is so the cards do not become tainted by another person's psychic energy.

The Importance of Ritual

Although there are many who hold with elaborate rituals and ceremonies when preparing a reading, it is generally recognized that such customs are not absolutely necessary. Formality of some kind is important, however, for two reasons. Firstly, a reading requires that the unconscious mind be brought to the fore, and this can only be done in a state of relaxation and quiet. If the reader or the person receiving the reading is overexcited, restless or nervous, then the intuitive, hidden parts of the mind will not be adequately prepared. In order to achieve the right conditions, small rituals and routines are invaluable—shuffling the cards in a certain order, for example, or lighting incense and saying a small prayer—calm the mind and create a better atmosphere. Secondly, Tarot combines random or chance factors with elements that are rigid and fixed, and in order to make sense of these properties there needs to be a solid framework to work within.

Environment

A Tarot reading should not be considered a spectator sport. Distractions, such as people talking or laughing, can turn a reading into a farce. Although it may be difficult to refuse giving a reading at a party or among a group of friends, the best results are always obtained by two people in a quiet room where they are able to concentrate their minds fully.

Selecting a Spread

If you have little or no previous experience of the Tarot it is important to begin with a spread that you are comfortable with and fully understand. In the following chapter the Celtic Cross Spread is explained. This is a fairly easy one to follow and many first time users of the Tarot find it very useful. Experience in handling the cards will build the necessary confidence to attempt more complex spreads, but it is always best to master one before tackling another.

Using a spread provides a framework that enables the reader to relate cards to specific areas of the enquirer's life. This means that each card in each position relates to a specific aspect of the enquirer's life. Often it may seem that a card has no relevance to the area indicated by its position in the spread. In such cases the general meaning of the card should be adapted to suit the position in which it appears in the spread. Thus a card that suggests difficulty in a relationship may, in a position where career matters are indicated, be taken as referring to difficulties in a working relationship.

Shuffling and Cutting

Before shuffling the cards, it is often suggested that a Significator be selected. This is a card that represents the person seeking a reading or the situation about which the advice is being sought. If the Significator is to represent a person then it should be chosen by the similarities in hair and eye colouring between that person and the card. If the Significator is to represent a situation then it should be a card which broadly describes the situation. If you do decide to use a Significator then it should be removed from the deck before shuffling and placed face up on the table.

The cards should be well shuffled before beginning the reading. If you intend to use reverse meanings then half the cards should be turned around and well dispersed through the pack. It is important that once the reversed cards are shuffled in the pack by the reader that they are not reversed again or the reading given will be upside down. Once shuffled by the reader the cards should be handed to the person seeking the reading for them to shuffle. The cards should then be handed back to the reader—all the time both parties taking care not to turn the pack around.

Selecting the Cards

There are two methods of selecting cards. One is for the reader to ask the other person to cut the deck twice using their left hand. Each time the top of the cut should be placed to the left of the bottom of the cut so that three piles are made. The three piles are then collected so that the cards originally on top go to the bottom. The reader then lays out the cards from the top of the pack in the chosen spread.

The second way is for the entire pack to be fanned out, face down across the table. The person seeking the reading should then select their cards, being careful to keep them in order. The first card should always remain on top of the pile of selected cards as this way it is easier to remember the order in which they were chosen.

Laying out the Cards

Once the cards are selected they should be laid out face down in their correct positions in the spread. Only when they are all correctly laid out should they be turned over—when turning them over it should be from side to side, not from end to end, as doing this will reverse the meanings. When interpreting the spread, the cards should be regarded as upright or reversed from the reader's point of view.

Before looking at each card individually it is a good idea to take some time to get an overall picture of the spread. If there is a predominance of Court cards or of cards from one suit then this can be significant. If there are a lot of Cups, then relationships and matters of the heart will probably be a dominant theme in the reading. Wands indicate that careers or other enterprises are likely to be important, Swords suggest some form of conflict or struggle, and Pentacles indicate practical affairs. A lot of Court cards together can mean that factors outwith the enquirer's control will shape their destiny and that the actions of other people will have an important influence on their lives.

Looking at the spread as a whole also makes it easier to relate cards to each other. This is an aspect of reading the Tarot which improves with experience and it can often be simpler for a beginner to wait until the end of a reading to make summing up remarks. In some spreads there are very obvious connections when certain cards next to each other develop one theme. For example, three cards in a row may mean 'the way forward', and are therefore intended to be interpreted together. Other cards may modify the meaning of the cards next to them, and more time and thought is required when interpreting them. The ability to assess relationships between cards comes with experience and familiarity, however, and the beginner cannot be expected to see in a spread all the things a more experienced reader may see.

The Celtic Cross Spread

The popular Celtic Cross Spread is most useful for obtaining
an answer to a specific question. To begin, the reader
selects a card to represent the person seeking the reading or
which best describes the matter about which an enquiry is
being made. This card is commonly called the Significator. If
the Significator is to represent the enquirer then the card
should be one which corresponds in some way to his or her
personal description. A Knight should be chosen if the
enquirer is a man aged over forty; a King should be chosen
if the man is under that age; a Queen if it is a woman over
forty; and a Page for a younger female.

The four Court cards in Wands represent very fair people,
with blond or auburn hair, fair complexion and blue eyes.
The Court cards in Cups signify people with light brown or
dull fair hair and grey or blue eyes. Those in Swords stand
for people having hazel or grey eyes, dark brown hair and
dull complexion. Lastly the Court cards in Pentacles refer to
persons with very dark brown or black hair, dark eyes and
sallow complexions. These allocations are not absolutely rigid,
however, and you should also be guided by the temperament
of the enquirer; a dark person may be exceptionally outgoing
and gregarious and would, therefore, be better represented by
a Sword card than a Pentacle. On the other hand, a very fair
subject who is quite easy-going and relaxed should be referred
to by Cups rather than Wands.

If it is decided that it is better to make the Significator
refer to the matter being asked into then the card which is

most closely associated with that area should be chosen. For example, if the question is to do with the success of a legal dispute, then the Justice card should be made the Significator.

Having selected the appropriate Significator, place it on the table, face upwards. Then shuffle and cut the rest of the pack in the normal Tarot manner, that is, three times, keeping the face of the cards downwards.

Turn up the top or **first card** of the pack and cover the Significator with it, saying, 'This covers him'. This card indicates the influence that is affecting the person or matter of the inquiry and gives an idea of the direction of the reading as a whole.

Turn up the **second card** and lay it across the first, saying, 'This crosses him'. This indicates the nature of the obstacles in the matter. If it is a favourable card, the opposing forces will not be serious, or it may indicate that something good in itself may not be productive of good in that particular connection.

Turn up the **third card** and place it above the Significator card, saying, 'This crowns him'. This card represents (a) the enquirer's aim or ideal or (b) the best that can be hoped for under the circumstances.

Turn up the **fourth card** and place it below the Significator and say, 'This is beneath him'. It shows the foundation or basis of the matter, that which has already happened and the relationship of the enquirer to that event.

Turn up the **fifth card** and place it on the side of the Significator from which he is looking. If the Significator is not a Court card and cannot, therefore, be said to be facing any particular way, then the reader must beforehand select the direction in which the card is said to be looking. Placing the card, say, 'This is beside him'. This indicates an influence which has passed or is passing away.

Turn up the **sixth card** and place it on the side that the Significator is facing and say, 'This is before him'. It shows an influence that is coming into action and will operate in the near future.

The cards are now disposed in the form of a cross, the Significator—covered by the first card—being in the centre.

The next four cards are turned up in succession and placed one above the other in a line on the right-hand side of the cross.

The first of these, or the **seventh card**, signifies the Significator—whether a person or a thing—and shows its position or attitude in the circumstances.

The **eighth card** signifies his house, that is, his environment and the tendencies at work therein which have an effect on the matter—for instance, his position in life, the influence of immediate friends, and so forth.

The **ninth card** gives his hopes or fears in the matter.

The **tenth card** is what will come, the final result, the culmination which is brought about by the influences shown by the other cards that have been shown in the reading.

It is on this card that the reader should concentrate all their intuitive faculties, taking into account all the divinatory meanings attached to it. In theory, this card should embody all else that has been gathered from the interpretations of the other cards.

The reading is now complete; but should the last card have not given up any conclusion then it might be worthwhile to repeat the operation, taking the tenth card as a Significator.

It is significant if in any reading the tenth card is a Court card. This indicates that the subject of the reading will be greatly influenced by the person represented by that card, and the outcome of anything troubling the enquirer may be dependent on his or her actions. If this is the case then more can be learned if the Court card is taken as the Significator in a fresh reading.

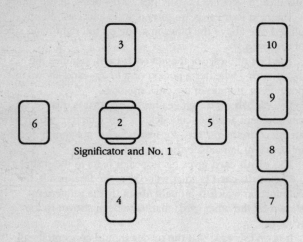

Significator and No. 1

The Significator

1 What covers him.
2 What crosses him.
3 What crowns him.
4 What is beneath him.
5 What is behind him.
6 What is before him.
7 Himself.
8 His house.
9 His hopes or fears.
10 What will come.

The Major Arcana

The Trumps

The twenty-two cards of the Major Arcana, also known as the Trump cards, signify underlying influences on one's life. These are circumstances which are out of human control and are more commonly referred to as fate or destiny. They also represent things which are not apparent in day-to-day life but which are hidden from view in the subconscious.

Many experts also see in the Major Arcana the journey of life, from the innocence and wonder of childhood, through tests and hardships to maturity, and then on to old age, death and spiritual transcendence. The cards reflect such a path in life by using universal symbolism. For example, the Empress and the Emperor as the protective mother and the guiding father respectively.

The Fool

This card shows an attractive young man in a carefree pose standing at the edge of a precipice. He often has his belongings on a stick over his shoulder and a dog by his side.

The Fool represents a carefree, relaxed and open attitude. It suggests the ability to live day by day without worrying about the future. The Fool also signifies childlike qualities such as trust and spontaneity.

Reversed Childishness and irresponsibility are indicated when the card appears reversed. It can therefore be taken as a warning to be more responsible and to have more thought for the consequences of one's actions.

The Magician

This card depicts a practitioner of the magical arts. A lemniscate, the symbol of infinity, is usually shown above his head.

One hand of the figure, gripping a wand, is pointing upwards to the heavens and the other is pointing down, signifying the drawing of power from a higher source and directing it towards practical, earthly matters. As well as signifying skill in directing energies, this card also indicates charm, articulacy and the ability to lead others.

Reversed The inability to turn thought into action is indicated here. This is due to poor leadership and communication skills and a lack of experience and confidence.

18

The High Priestess

The Priestess sits between two pillars that represent the pillars of Jerusalem, Boaz and Jakin. One is black, signifying the feminine characteristics of intuition and mystery, and the other white, representing the masculine principle of reason.

This card signifies guidance and wisdom of a spiritual or moral nature which comes from unconscious sources—intuition, dreams and fantasies.

Reversed The card can suggest a lack of inner harmony resulting from the suppression of feelings and the failure to acknowledge unconscious guidance. In a man's spread this reversed card signifies negative feelings towards women or that feminine qualities in himself are being ignored.

The Empress

This card shows a woman, often pregnant, sitting in a rich, fertile environment.

Unlike the High Priestess, who is virginal, the Empress represents motherhood and fertility. She also signifies physical and spiritual security and contentment in domestic situations and personal relationships. The benefits of this are generosity, kindness and the enjoyment of other people's company.

Reversed The Empress can also mean dissatisfaction with personal circumstances and a lack of material and emotional comfort. There could also be difficulties with physical health, particularly related to pregnancy and childbirth.

The Emperor

In contrast to the Empress, the Emperor sits in a hard and cold environment with a stern expression on his face.

This card represents masculine power and fatherly responsibility. In a reading it may indicate a connection to a position or figure of authority and could suggest that there is an opportunity to take control over others.

Reversed This indicates a problem connected with control, perhaps a dispute with a father or domineering husband or some other difficulty in a personal relationship. It also indicates a hostile attitude to authority and governance which may be nurturing resentment and rebellion.

The Hierophant

A Hierophant was an initiating priest in ancient Greece. He is depicted as giving advice to two figures in the foreground under his authority.

Originally this card signified the seeking of religious guidance, but in this secular age it represents all forms of guidance where the person giving advice is in a position of authority. Such authority figures include doctors, lawyers, professional counsellors, teachers and tutors. The card indicates that the advice given from such sources will be reliable and useful.

Reversed This indicates that advice given may not be reliable or that the nature of the problem is such that the advice is inappropriate.

The Lovers

Adam and Eve in the Garden of Eden are shown in this card with an angel looking down on them.

This card is not so much about love itself as about decision-making and commitment. The two lovers have their hands open and this signifies that the right decision will be made if there is careful thought and consultation. This applies to any major decision, such as getting married, moving house or changing job.

Reversed This is a warning against making a hasty decision or not making a decision at all and letting important issues go unresolved.

The Chariot

This card shows an upright warrior figure in a chariot with two sphinxes, one black, one white, in the foreground.

The rider represents self-determination and control. The sphinxes represent the opposing forces within human nature which have to be mastered before progress can be made. In a reading the card implies that with enough strength of purpose ambitions can be realized and obstacles overcome.

Reversed This is a warning against losing control and letting one of the two sphinxes gain dominance, thus pulling the rider off course. In order to regain control one has to be rational, assess the situation, and attempt to balance conflicting impulses.

Strength

This card shows a young woman taming a lion. She has a garland in her hair and around her waist.

The lion represents strong, negative emotions such as anger or jealousy and the woman moral strength and self-control. Together they show the importance of balance between these factors. A calm and rational approach in a situation where strong emotions may be aroused is urged.

Reversed Lack of self-belief, despair, and feelings of powerlessness are signified by the reversed card. These feelings can be overcome, however, if strong emotions are correctly channelled.

The Hermit

The Hermit is portrayed as an old man dressed in a habit and carrying a lantern. The barren background signifies isolation.

As the hermit has withdrawn from society, so the card signifies a need to withdraw and contemplate life. It also indicates a need to be more self-reliant and in control of events. This is especially true during times of worry or crisis. Help from others is unwelcome, however, as it is only through contemplation of one's own self that the strength to make progress can be found.

Reversed This indicates loneliness and self-pity. Instead of living in the past the card urges one to look forward and seek solutions to problems.

Wheel of Fortune

The Wheel of Fortune is shown
being turned by a sphinx, the
symbol of feminine wisdom.
Various animals are shown
around the wheel, representing
the Living Creatures of Ezekiel.

This card indicates fate and
events beyond human control.
In the upright position it
indicates good luck or the
optimistic outlook that things
will work out for the best. This
can also mean that one has a
fatalistic outlook on life, leaving
too much to chance and failing
to make decisions.

Reversed Usually this
indicates bad luck and events
out of one's control. It can also
signify that leaving things to
chance will be damaging.

Justice

Justice is depicted as a woman
on a throne with a sword in
one hand and a set of scales in
the other.

This card signifies a legal
matter and concern that justice
be done. If the card appears
upright in a reading then
reason and justice will prevail
and the issue will be resolved
fairly without recourse to
heated, emotional argument.

Reversed In this position the
card indicates unfairness, bias
and injustice. It may also
indicate that in a situation
where there is deadlock a
completely new approach is
required in order to make
progress.

The Hanged Man

Although the sight of a man hanging by one foot from a tree can be a little alarming, this card is not a bad omen.

The strange hanging figure represents self-sacrifice and dedication to a cause. Often those virtues are criticized and ridiculed by others who cannot see the end purpose. It can also mean a change in attitude or direction that is personally rewarding but misunderstood by others.

Reverse This signifies lack of purpose and apathy, often coming about through the misguided pursuit of illusory goals and the neglect of one's spiritual wellbeing. It is a call, therefore, to re-order one's priorities and pursue that which is truly rewarding.

Death

The skeleton on horseback is often seen as gruesome and frightening by those unfamiliar with the Tarot. Usually, however, this card signifies change rather than actual death, and the flag being carried aloft and the shining sun in the background are symbols of new life.

More specifically, the card indicates radical change and renewal with one phase of life ending and a new one beginning. With change there is also some grief for things that are lost, and this has to be faced up to and overcome.

Reverse This signifies resistance to change and fear of the future. It may be that changes made in one's life are more traumatic the more one holds on to the past.

Temperance

This card depicts a winged figure pouring liquid from one chalice to another. One foot is on land while the other is in water, symbolizing equilibrium and balance in nature.

Temperance in a reading signifies good self-control and a balanced personality. It also suggests that balance and caution may be required in a situation, particularly if that situation involves arbitrating between two other parties.

Reversed Imbalance and uncertainty are indicated by this card. This brings unhappiness, mood swings and self-doubt, and in dealings with other people this emotional instability means inconsistency and clumsiness.

The Devil

A card that is often misinterpreted. The Devil figure does *not* mean evil, lust and demonic possession. Rather it signifies unpleasant emotions, which all of us experience from time to time, such as anger, frustration and bitterness.

The figures chained to the plinth symbolize being stuck in an uncomfortable situation. The card suggests that feelings of helplessness can be defeated, however, and that possibly there may be solutions to the situation that have not yet been explored.

Reversed This means much the same as the upright card, although it can also mean that a bad situation has been allowed to go unchallenged for too long.

THE TOWER.

THE STAR.

The Tower

This card depicts a tower being destroyed by a thunderbolt and the inhabitants falling to earth. A crown is usually shown being blown off the top of the flaming tower.

This card represents an unexpected blow to the ego or pride, which at first can seem humiliating and damaging. In the long term, however, it proves to be a useful experience from which lessons can be learned. It can also mean a physical injury, which, again, is not as damaging as it first appears.

Reversed This signifies some misfortune or unpleasant event, which could have been avoided or which has been allowed to develop over a period of time. In a sense, therefore, the resultant injury is self-inflicted.

The Star

The Goddess of the Stars appears naked, pouring two jugs of water, one on the earth and one into a pool. The setting is serene and peaceful, and the sky is filled with one large star and seven smaller ones.

This card indicates peace, contentment and wellbeing. This can come after a period of turmoil and so represents a return to physical and spiritual health. New beginnings and fresh experiences may be ahead.

Reversed This indicates the opportunity for rest and repair, an opportunity that may not yet be realized. The reversed card, therefore, is a sign of hope and an encouragement to someone feeling anxiety or self-doubt.

THE MOON.

THE SUN.

The Moon

This card shows a dog and a wolf howling at a moon which has a female profile within. A path leads from the sea, between two dark towers, to the horizon. A lobster is seen emerging from the sea.

This card represents confusion and lack of direction. The lobster symbolizes unconscious fears of failure and despair, and the dog and wolf represent aspects of our animal nature that may do us harm. The woman's face on the moon is associated with delusion and deception.

Reversed Morbid fantasizing and feelings of utter despair may have become a serious problem—it is time to confide in a friend and seek support.

The Sun

This card depicts a small boy riding a white horse while the sun, with a masculine face, gazes down.

The Sun symbolizes success, happiness and personal achievement. In a reading this card indicates the possession of energy, optimism and high ideals, and it bodes well for the eventual fulfilment of ambitions. There is also a sense given of enjoyment and fun in the pursuit of one's goals.

Reversed This indicates a gap between personal plans and ambitions and the present reality. More effort, planning and dedication are needed. At the same time it is important to guard against feelings of despondency.

Judgement

This card depicts the dead rising from their graves at the call of an angel's trumpet, in Biblical terms, the Day of Judgement.

This card signifies self-assessment. In the upright position it is a positive appraisal and there is an acceptance of the past and a sense of satisfaction and achievement. The future can therefore be faced openly and without fear.

Reversed The card still signifies change, except that when looking back there is regret and remorse and a feeling of dissatisfaction with the way things turned out. This self-condemnation is damaging and usually unwarranted. It is far better to accept what has happened and move on.

The World

This card features a dancing woman surrounded by a laurel wreath in the centre and an angel, a bull, an eagle and a lion in the four corners.

This card represents the successful completion of a project or the happy conclusion of a phase in life. As well as a sense of fulfilment and contentment, there is a much deeper, spiritual sense of self-awareness and understanding.

Reversed In this position the card indicates a circle of frustration and boredom. A new approach is needed to break free of the cycle. It can also signify delays to the completion of a project or phase in life which may be frustrating and holding back personal development.

The Minor Arcana

The fifty-six cards of the Minor Arcana consist of four suits: Wands, Cups, Swords and Pentacles. There are 40 numbered, or 'Pip' cards, and 16 Court cards. The four suits represent the elements: the suit of Wands is associated with fire, Cups with water, Swords with air, and Pentacles with earth. The meanings of each card relate to the qualities displayed by each of these elements.

The Pip Cards

Unlike the cards of the Major Arcana, which relate to spiritual matters, the Pip cards represent everyday circumstances and events and how people feel about them.

For ease of reference the cards have been grouped by their numerical values rather then by their suits. The significance of the numbers is outlined below:

The Aces
The Aces represent two things. As a whole, they signify singularity or the unity of several components; individually they represent the elements of fire (Wands), water (Cups), air (Swords) and earth (Pentacles).

The Twos
The Twos represent the relationship between two entities. This can be a personal relationship or the relationship between two loyalties, emotions or impulses.

The Threes
The Threes represent the concept of creation and symbolize

the product that results from some form of union, for example, a child. They also represent the link between two opposing forces and are associated with fate and divinity.

The Fours
Four is the number of the material world, representing the four elements and the four dimensions. As it is strongly associated with nature and matter it indicates stability and order.

The Fives
The stability and order of four is disrupted by the addition of one to make five. It is the number of disorder and confusion and indicates the arrival of difficult times.

The Sixes
Six is the number of days in the Creation so it represents completion and fulfilment. It also indicates reward for efforts and justice.

The Sevens
Seven is considered to be a magical or lucky number and is associated with virtue and wisdom.

The Eights
As four and two are the most stable numbers, their multiplication to give eight means that number indicates success, progress and personal development.

The Nines
Nine is three times three, so it contains the creative force of that number tripled. It also indicates the final stages of creation and the reaping of rewards.

The Tens
Ten represents a new stage in development as well as being the number of completion. It can also be seen as 'just enough', where one more brings in destruction or decadence.

The Court Cards

The Court cards in the Minor Arcana usually consist of a Page, a Knight, a Queen and a King. These cards are generally thought to represent particular individuals and can be seen as the person having the reading, people known to them, or people they are going to meet.

Each kind of Court card represents a particular kind of person, and the suit they appear in indicates what distinctive personality traits they have:

The Pages

A Page represents a child, either a boy or a girl, or a young woman. All the Pages are associated with the earth element, signifying practical matters, organization and planning.

The Knights

Usually depicted on horseback, the Knights represent youth, progress and energy. All the Knights correspond to the element of fire and the fiery spirit is present to some degree in all of them.

The Queens

The Queens represent mature women. If the person consulting the cards is female, however, it can often refer to them. The associated element is water, indicating gentleness and other traditionally feminine qualities.

The Kings

The Kings represent mature men. As with the Queens, if the person consulting the cards is male it can often refer to them. The element associated with Kings is air, which indicates authority, rationality, and other traditionally male qualities.

ACE of WANDS.

ACE of CUPS.

Ace of Wands

This card shows a hand appearing from a cloud, gripping a stout club.

It is a strongly masculine image indicating creativity, virility, enthusiasm, excitement, personal growth and ambition. It is a particularly promising card to receive if starting out on a new venture as it shows that the ability and creativity are there to make it a success.

Reversed A misdirection of energies is indicated, and there are feelings of frustration, weakness and apathy. However, some of the elements of the upright reading are still present, and things could be turned around with self-discipline and organization.

Ace of Cups

An open hand is shown in this card holding a chalice from which four streams of water are falling. There is also a dove descending to place a wafer in the chalice.

This card represents the feminine element of water and is associated with love, relationships and emotional growth. It shows that there is openness, contentment, and fulfilment in a relationship. Specifically, it could indicate a marriage or a pregnancy.

Reversed This indicates sadness and despondency. The water represents tears brought about by feelings of loneliness and a lack of security. There may also be an end to, or a disappointment within, a relationship.

Ace of Swords

This card shows a hand gripping a sword, the point of which is encircled by a crown.

This is a card of great forcefulness and represents the ability to think clearly and rationally. It also stands for justice and authority and can signify legal matters or some other dispute where clear thinking and decision making is required.

Specifically, it could mean that there is a sense of fulfilment when a correct decision has been made or when there has been a favourable outcome to some dispute.

Reversed This indicates feelings of frustration with what is felt to be an unfair decision or situation.

Ace of Pentacles

A hand from the clouds holds a pentacle in this card. Beneath there is a garden scene and a mountain can be seen through a gap in the hedge.

This card stands for fulfilment and stability in personal, physical, or material terms and a sense of total contentment with one's present situation.

Reversed This can indicate an unhealthy preoccupation with material gain, a poor home life, unstable relationships, bad health, or worry about financial matters. It may also show that for some reason there is a lack of enjoyment of life and an inability to see the good aspects of one's situation.

Two of Wands

A man is shown in this card with a globe in one hand and a staff in the other. He looks out to sea from a battlement which has a second staff fixed to it.

Wands are associated with careers, ambition and creative energy. This card indicates that some kind of crossroads has been reached and that a decision is called for. It suggests that this may be the time for assessment and planning.

Reversed This indicates some loss of momentum brought about by self-doubt and a feeling that personal achievements have not been as valuable as had previously been thought. There may also be a sense of anticlimax and a falling out with work colleagues.

Two of Cups

The couple shown in this card are pledging one another and above their raised chalices there is a lion's head supported by a pair of giant wings.

This card represents a love affair, a marriage, a business partnership, or a close friendship, and indicates that this relationship is of particular importance as there may be a need for support during a difficult time.

Reversed This represents problems in a once close relationship. This could mean an argument or conflict of some kind or it could mean distrust and a sense of betrayal. It also indicates that decisions regarding the long-term future of a relationship are best left for a time.

Two of Swords

In this card a blindfolded woman balances two very long swords on her shoulders.

This indicates that there is some sort of power struggle going on or the breakdown of a once close relationship and that there is a need for a balanced and rational approach to the problem. Self-restraint and caution against making rash decisions is indicated.

Reversed This card represents a tense situation which has become intolerable. Either one or both sides in the dispute are now venting their true feelings and there is little hope for reconciliation while both parties remain in this frame of mind.

Two of Pentacles

This card shows a young man dancing with a pentacle in each hand. The two pentacles are linked by an endless cord.

A balanced and progressive attitude towards the practical matters of everyday life is indicated here. Any problems which come up are easily dealt with and any setbacks which occur are soon forgotten. There is a general feeling of contentment and optimism.

Reversed A lack of balance is indicated and there is likely to be inconstancy and impatience in one's actions, mood swings, uncertainty, and periods of self-doubt which impede progress on many levels. There is also a recklessness and immaturity in some behaviour which is damaging.

Three of Wands

This card shows a male figure
with his back turned standing
between three staffs. He is
looking out over a sea view and
ships can be seen passing by.

Some form of creative
initiative is indicated here. It
may be related to a business
venture, but it could also apply
to a new career or lifestyle.
Progress is very much
dependent on luck, although
there has been a good start
made and there is every reason
to be optimistic for the future.

Reversed This card indicates
indecision, lack of confidence,
and procrastination. No
progress is being made and
good opportunities which may
not come again are being
missed.

Three of Cups

Three cheerful young women
are shown in this card lifting
their chalices to each other.
Around their feet lie different
vegetables and fruits.

A creative force within the
emotional realm is indicated as
being very much to the fore by
this card. This may signify a
new relationship, a marriage, or
the birth of a child.
Alternatively, it could mean a
period of spiritual, psychic, or
artistic growth.

Reversed Intolerance and
selfishness in a relationship are
indicated by this card and a
potentially good situation is
being spoiled as a result.
Divorce, domestic problems,
argument and exploitation of
another's goodwill are all
indicated here.

Three of Swords

This card shows three swords piercing a heart. Storm clouds are gathered in the background.

Three may sometimes be an unfortunate number as it can mean conflict, aggression and the escalation of problems. There are also similarities with the Death card of the Major Arcana in that changes which may be good in the long term are very painful and difficult to face up to in the short term.

Reversed This indicates that a difficult and painful period of transition is likely to have lasted for a long time. This has led to conflict, argument and destructive practices being entered into out of a sense of frustration.

Three of Pentacles

A sculptor is shown at work here in a monastery while a monk and another hooded figure look on.

This card represents creativity, hard work and long-term rewards. There is a feeling that one's efforts and energies are being meaningfully employed and are helping other people. This is recognized and appreciated, which is also very satisfying.

Reversed This indicates that there is frustration because hard work and effort are not being recognized or rewarded as much as they should be. Often there is criticism and this further undermines confidence in personal ability and leaves a feeling of being taken for granted.

Four of Wands

In this card four staves hold aloft a garland. Two female figures stand in the background with nosegays in their hands and behind them is a castle and a bridge going over a moat.

Artistic expression and creative impulses being pursued in a calculated, methodical way in a stable and secure environment are indicated here. It can also indicate a rewarding holiday or a change in environment that bring new experiences and broaden the mind.

Reversed This indicates a situation where there are restrictions on creativity and self-expression in the form of rules and regulations. This is causing unhappiness and resentment.

Four of Cups

An unhappy young man sits beneath a tree in this card. He is contemplating three cups laid before him while a fourth is offered by a hand appearing from a cloud.

An underlying feeling of being in a rut is indicated, and there is little value placed in the good things one actually has. New experiences and situations are craved, which will stimulate and excite.

Reversed This indicates that boredom has become overly indulgent self-pity. It is possible that there are problems with reliance on alcohol, drugs or food. If so, then help must be sought to overcome the problem.

Four of Swords

This card shows a knight lying upon his tomb. Three swords are on the wall and one by his side.

This indicates a period of recovery from an illness or a period of contemplation after a difficult time, perhaps after a bereavement. It can also simply mean that it is time to 'get away from it all' and enjoy a well-earned holiday.

Reversed Feelings of being isolated and ignored are indicated by this card. This may result from illness or because friends have moved away or distanced themselves in some other way. It could also mean that a certain situation has been left behind but feelings of regret or resentment remain.

Four of Pentacles

This card shows a crowned figure gripping one pentacle tightly and resting his feet on two more. A fourth pentacle rests on his crown.

A very solid domestic situation is indicated. There is great resistance to any form of change, which can be very good if it follows a period of hardship and struggle. It can also be very limiting, as after a time the situation may become too predictable and safe.

Reversed This is often said to be the miser's card, as it indicates a reluctance to give anything up. This can apply to a relationship, career, or any other aspect of life. A fear of failure is probably the root cause and this should be addressed.

Five of Wands

This card shows five youths
playfully brandishing staves in
mimic warfare.

Optimism and energy are
indicated here. Little
annoyances and minor setbacks
are also indicated, but these
should be regarded as
interesting challenges to be met
and overcome. This can
actually be very satisfying for
the enquirer, adding excitement
to his or her life.

Reverse This indicates that
the obstacles and setbacks are
more serious in nature and that
there is very little enjoyment to
be had from them. There is also
likely to be conflict and
argument, possibly with one
person who aims to disrupt
another's plans.

Five of Cups

A dark, cloaked figure
dominates this card. He is
looking sideways at three
prone cups. Two more cups
stand upright behind him.

This card indicates
unhappiness with the way
some event has gone and a
feeling of missed opportunity.
Dwelling on what might have
been is a futile exercise,
however, and it is far better to
accept things and move on.

Reversed The feelings of loss
indicated by this card are more
serious. It may be that someone
or something very important
has gone. This could mean an
actual bereavement, in which
case these feelings will persist
until one comes to term with
the loss.

Five of Swords

This card shows a young man with a disdainful look on his face gathering up swords. Two other dejected figures are shown retreating from the field.

A sense of humiliation and defeat is indicated here. A personal weakness may have been revealed, or there may have been a conflict with a domineering person, which has resulted in exposure to ridicule. This is only a minor setback as it is probably only pride that has been hurt.

Reverse This indicates that more lasting damage has been done and that some form of betrayal, dishonesty or trickery has been involved. It may be that one person has been the cause of this upset, who is too powerful to be challenged.

Five of Pentacles

Two pathetic-looking figures, poorly dressed and apparently homeless, are shown on this card. Snow lies on the ground around them as they pass by a stained glass window.

Unemployment, financial difficulties, or the absence of love or security are indicated here. The problem may be alleviated, however, by the support of another party, perhaps a close friend.

Reversed This indicates an acute awareness of a bad situation. Poverty, domestic insecurity or unemployment may be signified, or there may be a general feeling of insecurity stemming from a lack of love or companionship. Things will only get worse if help is not sought to remedy the situation.

Six of Wands

This card shows a horseman with a staff in his hand which is adorned with a laurel crown. Footmen bearing staves are at his side.

Success and achievement in some enterprise is indicated here. A lot of energy and effort has probably been directed towards some end result and now that that commitment has paid off, it is time for celebrating and enjoying the fruits of one's labour.

Reverse This indicates that the completion of some project has been delayed or has gone without the proper recognition. Expected news may also have been delayed due to some misunderstanding or lack of proper communication.

Six of Cups

Two children are shown here, innocently playing in an old garden. They have filled six cups with flowers.

This is a card of the past and memories. It can indicate reward for past efforts and recognition for acts of kindness. It may also mean that reminiscing about the past will bring pleasure or that perhaps an old friend or lover will return unexpectedly to pay back a kindness or lend a hand in time of need.

Reverse This indicates being haunted by an unhappy past to the extent that the present cannot be fully enjoyed. It can also signify a reluctance to face up to changes in a relationship or in a domestic situation.

Six of Swords

This card shows a ferryman carrying passengers in his punt across calm waters.

Getting away from a bad situation is the theme of this card. This may be a slow and difficult process, and should be planned far in advance and adequately prepared for. It can also indicate a holiday or a move to a new job or home.

Reverse This indicates that a solution to some problem is only temporary and that a permanent solution has been avoided. Taking the easy way out may suffice in the short term, but eventually the problem will resurface and might be even more difficult to deal with.

Six of Pentacles

A well-dressed merchant is shown here weighing money in a pair of scales and distributing it to two beggars.

Fairness and balance with regard to money and possessions are indicated by this card. This may indicate charitable feelings and the need to 'put something back' into society. Generally, the enquirer is likely to be generous by nature and a person who gets pleasure from helping others.

Reversed This indicates a feeling of being taken for granted and not getting proper recognition. The situation may seem unfair, as if one person has been doing all the giving and another all the taking. It may also indicate theft of money or possessions.

Seven of Wands

This card shows a young man balanced on a craggy eminence brandishing a staff, apparently in self-defence.

This card signifies great personal ability, determination and energy. A test that calls for a supreme effort is indicated, perhaps an interview for a job or an examination of some sort. There is nothing to indicate failure, and there will probably be satisfaction in being able to handle such a situation well.

Reverse A challenge may prove to be too much, although it is more likely through lack of confidence than of ability that they will fail. Self-doubt is holding back the true expression of ability and that needs to be addressed.

Seven of Cups

In this card a silhouetted figure contemplates seven strange visions that have appeared before him.

This card suggests that choices have to be made carefully with regard to future goals and ideals. There may be a tendency to fantasize about future achievements. Those that are unrealistic must be separated from those worth pursuing—a process that calls for rational analysis.

Reversed Confusion and uncertainty are indicated by this card. There may be too many choices and possibilities for an easy decision to be made. Deluding oneself with unrealistic and unattainable dreams and fantasies is also indicated.

Seven of Swords

This card shows a young man apparently in the act of stealing five swords. Two more swords remain in the ground and a camp is nearby.

The chance to use one's intelligence to deal with a problem in a clever and skilful way is indicated. There may be some tricky opposition to face, but with cunning and guile they will be defeated. An unorthodox and unusual approach will often pay off.

Reversed This card indicates a reluctance to take chances or make pre-emptive moves to solve a problem or break a deadlock. Timidity, conventionalism, and fear of ridicule and failure only serve to prolong difficulties however.

Seven of Pentacles

The young man in this card rests his head and looks intently at seven pentacles attached to a clump of greenery.

This card indicates that sustained effort will bring the results hoped for. There is also the suggestion that a stroke of luck will progress matters.

Reversed This indicates a feeling of despondency and an inclination to abandon a project which is not progressing. It may be that mistakes have been made along the way which have put the end hoped for in jeopardy and which cannot be rectified. It is probably best to accept defeat and move on to something new.

Eight of Wands

This card shows eight staffs in flight across open country.

Progress towards a satisfactory conclusion of any matter at hand is indicated here. There will be no more delays or hold-ups and things which have long been hoped for will start to happen.

Reversed This indicates that there is confusion and uncertainty as things are not going the way they are supposed to. Lack of organization and planning, and an inability to cope with a complex situation, mean that although there is much activity and effort, little is actually achieved.

Eight of Cups

A dejected-looking man is shown in this card walking away from two rows of cups.

This card indicates that something very important is missing from one's life. There may be a good degree of emotional and material stability in the present situation, but a need to find a deeper level of contentment is constantly nagging. A drastic change in lifestyle may be called for to satisfy this longing.

Reversed This indicates uncertainty with future plans and a need to give things some serious thought. It may be that there is dissatisfaction with the present situation but very little idea of what one can do to change things.

Eight of Swords

This card portrays a young woman, bound and blindfolded, surrrounded by upright swords.

A desire to make changes and improve certain aspects of one's life is indicated here. For the time being, however, only small improvements are likely to succeed. This may be frustrating, but effort and perseverence will pay off in the future.

Reversed Feelings of being hemmed in and held back are stronger when the card is reversed. However, the situation is unlikely to get any worse, and if some small changes can be initiated now then later developments may be more kind.

Eight of Pentacles

This card shows a young stonemason at his work, the results of which he exhibits in the form of trophies.

Prosperity and personal satisfaction are indicated here, and there is a strong sense of achievement and pride derived from the exercise of one's own particular skills. This feeling may come from work well done or from some hobby or sporting achievement.

Reversed A problem with long-term goals and the frustration of personal ambitions are indicated here. Worries about money and short term security mean that too much time is spent on small and transitory gains that detract from working towards bigger goals.

Nine of Wands

This card shows a young man with an expectant look on his face leaning upon his staff. Eight other staffs are lined up behind him.

Rewards and benefits stemming from past deeds are indicated here. Hardships and struggles in the past, which have built resilience and character, are now being acknowledged. A more balanced, cautious and mature approach to life's problems has also developed.

Reversed This indicates a stubborness and defensiveness stemming from bad experiences in the past. This undermines any attempt to progress with something new or different, and it is a problem that needs to be addressed.

Nine of Cups

A well-contented man resting after a feast is central in this card. Behind him, a counter holds nine cups, which are probably full of wine.

A general feeling of wellbeing and contentment in domestic affairs is indicated by this card. Generosity and unselfishness abound, and sharing this happiness with friends and family brings a great deal of satisfaction.

Reversed This card indicates complacency, false optimism, and poor judgement. Everything may not be as it seems—situations may not be as secure or friendships as close as assumed.

Nine of Swords

In this card a figure sits upright in bed, head in hands. Nine swords hover menacingly above the bed.

A preoccupation with past experiences, particularly those that were painful, is indicated here. There is anxiety about what other people think and say about you. There is also a fear of the future and an inability to relax, which may cause sleeplessness and depression.

Reversed This card indicates that the depression is more intense and persistent. There is also suspicion of other people being unfair or cruel. In such a situation help from others is required and may be the only way to improve matters.

Nine of Pentacles

A young woman is shown here standing among an abundance of grapevines. A bird rests on her wrist.

This card indicates that the pursuit of some goal has been successful and the fruits of one's labours can now be enjoyed. The pursuit may not have been easy, however, and this makes the final outcome all the more enjoyable. This card also indicates someone who lives alone and who enjoys his or her personal achievements in solitude.

Reversed This indicates insecurity and fear that achievements may be undermined by past deeds. It also suggests a dependency on another person and a sharing of the credit for some achievement.

Ten of Wands

A man struggling to carry the ten staves held in his arms is shown here.

This card indicates over-burdening with responsibilities and commitments. There is a sense of oppression, which is causing unhappiness and distress. It may be that pride is standing in the way of delegation, but if the workload is not shared then everything may prove to be too much.

Reversed This indicates that more may have been taken on than can be handled. This has led to tiredness, confusion and an increasing inefficiency. It is time to re-evaluate the situation and prioritize commitments, perhaps giving up some responsibilities.

Ten of Cups

This card shows a man and woman standing in awe of a rainbow, which holds the ten cups. Two children are playing happily by their side.

This card indicates fulfilment and contentment within the context of a family or group of close friends. There may also be the less favourable interpretation that one of the group or family is not as happy as the others.

Reversed This indicates that someone or something is disrupting an otherwise idyllic situation. If it is a person then it may not necessarily be his or her fault. It could be that the other members of the group or family are neglecting them and not paying attention to his or her needs.

Ten of Swords

A prostrate figure is shown here, pierced by all the swords of the card.

This card indicates that caution should be shown when getting involved in a new venture, especially if it means trusting people whom you don't know. It also signifies the conclusion of something that has caused a great deal of pain and suffering. In a business venture or relationship this may mean that the crisis point has been reached and that things can only improve.

Reversed This indicates that the crisis point has not yet been reached, so preparations should be made for further trouble. Again, caution should be shown when dealing with a group of people.

Ten of Pentacles

This card shows a man and woman standing under an archway with a child by their side. Two dogs are also seen in the foreground being petted by an old man.

This card stands for family support—in both an emotional and a financial sense. Everyone benefits from this system of support if everyone plays an equal role and gives as much as he or she takes. Financial benefits from family connections are also indicated, perhaps an inheritance.

Reversed This card indicates that family and friends may be more of a hindrance than a help, stifling individuality and giving advice that has not been sought. There may also be problems with an inheritance.

Page of Wands

Personality

This card shows a confident, upright, young man surveying the land around him.

An energetic, lively, and resourceful personality is indicated. He or she is a good and reliable friend, and may also be the bearer of good news.

Reversed A self-centred personality with a tendency to gossip and spread hurtful rumours is indicated. He or she cannot be trusted with a secret.

Situation

This card indicates involvement in new and challenging ventures. A high level of enthusiasm and commitment is called for.

Reversed Bad news, or the delay of good news is indicated. Apathy and a lack of energy or ideas may also be signified.

Page of Cups

Personality

The young man in this card intently studies a fish rising from his chalice.

This indicates an imaginative and studious personality with a good deal of charm and a natural modesty.

Reversed A lazy, wasteful person lacking in direction and willpower is indicated.

Situation

This signifies that there are hidden talents which are now being discovered. Study and reflection are also indicated as being beneficial at this time.

Reversed Certain talents and skills are underutilized, and good opportunities for self-improvement may be being ignored or missed.

PAGE of SWORDS.

PAGE of PENTACLES.

Page of Swords

Personality
This card shows a lively young man holding a sword in an upright position.

An intelligent and capable personality is indicated. He or she is always thorough about things and may also at times be cautious and mistrustful.

Reversed This indicates a very cunning and manipulative person who uses other people and situations to advantage.

Situation
Clear thinking and caution are called for. All proposals should be carefully considered before a decision is made.

Reversed This indicates an environment of suspicion and mistrust, which cannot be allowed to persist. A problem needs to be tackled head-on.

Page of Pentacles

Personality
The youthful figure in this card looks intently at the pentacle that hovers above his outstretched hands.

This card indicates a steady and dependable personality with qualities that can always be relied upon. He or she could be a student or an apprentice.

Reversed A pompous and dull person is indicated who can frequently be obstructive and unhelpful.

Situation
This card indicates a working environment with a fixed routine that is very boring. It may only be temporary.

Reversed This card indicates unhappiness and frustration caused by a tedious and dull job or lifestyle.

KNIGHT of WANDS.

KNIGHT of CUPS.

Knight of Wands

Personality
This card shows a confident young man astride a fast-moving horse.

This indicates an attractive, adventurous personality, although there may be a tendency towards wild and unpredictable behaviour.

Reversed A reckless, unreliable personality, always stirring up trouble and disrupting things. Also impatient, never finishing anything of worth.

Situation
This card indicates involvement in new and challenging ventures. Holidays, adventures and lifestyle changes are likely.

Reversed A difficult and stressful time is indicated. A disastrous holiday or an unwise career move may be signified.

Knight of Cups

Personality
A graceful young man on a well-controlled horse is shown in this card.

A sensitive and imaginative personality is indicated here. There may be a tendency, however, to indulge in fantasy rather than apply ideas practically.

Reversed This indicates a personality who is not as pleasant as he or she first appears and may have something to hide.

Situation
Love, romance, and new relationships are indicated. There may also be opportunities for artistic expression.

Reversed Indicates unforeseen difficulties in a seemingly favourable situation.

Knight of Swords

Personality

A determined young man rides into battle in this card.

This indicates an intelligent, courageous, loyal and trustworthy personality. He or she is very capable in demanding situations and makes a strong ally.

Reversed This indicates an aggressive, impatient personality, often in conflict with others, who wastes energies and creates problems.

Situation

A period of some difficulty is indicated. The outcome will be favourable if a firm line is taken.

Reversed This indicates that in the difficult times ahead a hot-headed approach will only cause greater problems.

Knight of Pentacles

Personality

The young rider in this card sits astride a heavy horse and surveys what is ahead.

A practical and dependable personality is indicated. He or she will always work hard to get what is wanted.

Reversed A very conservative, dull and plodding character is indicated who frequently displays great stubbornness.

Situation

The time has come to slow down and relax. Steady progress will still be made.

Reversed This card indicates that little progress is being made towards what is desired and that the situation has become stagnant and boring. A change in approach is needed.

Queen of Wands

This card shows a confident, capable woman with an open outlook.

A sociable, active and resourceful woman who can direct her energies in several directions effectively is indicated. Outgoing and generous, she is a good wife and mother, and has many friends and interests. She will also have a good family life and be successful in business.

Reversed This card represents someone who thinks she is efficient and organized and who likes to be in control. This may be mistaken for arrogance, however, by those who resent her domineering and interfering attitude. She may think that others cannot manage without her.

Queen of Cups

The woman shown here appears rather self-absorbed as she contemplates a very elaborate chalice.

A quiet, reserved woman who keeps a lot concealed and so has an air of mystery about her is indicated. She is attractive and makes friends easily, but at times her personality may be hard to fathom. She is kind, intuitive and sympathetic, and her artistic and psychic skills are likely to be very highly developed.

Reversed This card indicates an impractical, frivolous woman, much given to self-deception and fantasizing. She may be rather vain and self-interested, with few real friends to count on in times of need.

Queen of Swords

With a rather stern expression on her face, this woman raises her weapon in her right hand and rests the hilt on the arm of her throne.

This card represents an intelligent, independent and strong-willed person who may be very ambitious. Traditionally a widow, she can also be a woman living alone who is divorced or separated. Despite her strength and independence, however, there is a degree of loneliness and a need for companionship.

Reversed This indicates a very cold and domineering woman. Her hard exterior conceals an inner loneliness, however, and she uses her coldness as a form of self-defence.

Queen of Pentacles

This card shows a reflective woman sitting on a throne in a very fertile and nurturing environment.

A loving, sensuous, open-hearted woman who likes to create a good atmosphere around herself is indicated. She is a good wife and mother who enjoys her domestic security and likes to share what she has with others. She also appreciates beautiful things and loves nature and animals.

Reversed This card indicates a woman who is obsessed with material worth. She is often suspicious and jealous of others. Underneath the unpleasant exterior, however, there may be a very insecure person who craves love and attention.

King of Wands

This card shows an alert and capable man sitting on a throne decorated with lion motifs.

An intelligent, fair-minded man who is able to see other people's point of view is indicated here. He is good at giving advice and resolving disputes amicably. A considerate husband and father, he is generous to others, dependable and affectionate.

Reversed This represents an intolerant man who can be very narrow-minded and critical of others. He always believes that he knows best and is often accused of being patronizing. He appears to be incapable of listening to anyone else's point of view and as a result is often accused of being insensitive and unsympathetic.

King of Cups

The figure in this card sits on a throne surrounded by the sea. A dolphin is leaping out of the water on one side and a ship passes by on the other.

This card indicates a cultured, sophisticated, well-educated man. He may be rather difficult to fathom at times, but a cool and competent exterior could be hiding emotional difficulties. He may be afraid of intimacy and, although supportive of those close to him, be slow to demonstrate affection.

Reversed This card represents someone who cannot be trusted, especially in business. He may use his superior education and privileged social contacts to take advantage of others and deceive people who thought themselves friends.

King of Swords

This figure appears to be sitting in judgement. His sword is held aloft, and a stern expression suggests a cold efficiency.

A powerful, strong-willed man who is well suited to a position of authority is indicated. He is fiercely independent, does not like being constrained in any way, and enjoys trying out new ideas and innovations. His rationality and ambition take him to the top of his profession.

Reversed This represents a very unpleasant character who can be dangerous to know and is best avoided in all walks of life. He is intelligent and independent but also a bully, cruel and unkind to those around him and exploitative of those weaker than himself.

King of Pentacles

This card shows a relaxed and confident man sitting on his throne in a flourishing garden.

A good, honest, hard-working man who has achieved stability and security through his own efforts is indicated. He may be well off, but money has never been an important motive for his actions. His tastes are simple, and he enjoys the good things in life. He may be skilled with his hands and has a talent for solving practical problems.

Reversed This represents a weak person who pursues, but cannot find pleasure or satisfaction in, material things. He may take out his frustrations on other people.

Key Words

The Trumps

The Fool *Upright*: innocence, trust, openness
Reversed: recklessness, irresponsibility

The Magician *Upright*: ability, confidence, communication
Reversed: lack of ability, poor communication

The Empress *Upright*: fulfilment, contentment, motherhood
Reversed: insecurity, discomfort, hardship

The Emperor *Upright*: authority, responsibility
Reversed: inferiority, resentment, frustration

The Hierophant *Upright*: advice, learning, teaching
Reversed: misinformation, bad advice

The Lovers *Upright*: commitment, decision, choice
Reversed: procrastination, bad decision

The Chariot *Upright*: empowerment, drive, ambition
Reversed: conflict, misdirection

Justice *Upright*: reason, fairness
Reversed: injustice, bias, unfairness

The Hermit *Upright*: solitariness, independence
Reversed: exclusion, self-pity

Wheel of Fortune *Upright*: chance, luck, optimism
Reversed: misfortune, pessimism

Strength *Upright*: inner balance, strength, control
Reversed: helplessness, imbalance

The Hanged Man *Upright*: perseverance, sacrifice
Reversed: apathy, dissatisfaction

Death *Upright*: change, renewal, rebirth
Reversed: delay, indecision

Temperance	*Upright*: balance, caution, arbitration *Reversed*: clumsiness, uncertainty
The Devil	*Upright*: anger, resentment, helplessness *Reversed*: suffering, despair
The Tower	*Upright*: misfortune, accident, humiliation *Reversed*: procrastination, self-injury
The Star	*Upright*: calm, healing, renewal, recovery *Reversed*: delay, prolongation
The Moon	*Upright*: confusion, turmoil, deception *Reversed*: fear, despair, helplessness
The Sun	*Upright*: optimism, ambition, success *Reversed*: impatience, frustration
Judgement	*Upright*: self-assessment, progression *Reversed*: regret, remorse, dissatisfaction
The World	*Upright*: completion, fulfilment *Reversed*: delay, frustration

Wands

Ace of Wands	*Upright*: creativity, energy, ambition *Reversed*: frustration, apathy
Two of Wands	*Upright*: assessment, planning, decision *Reversed*: self-doubt, anti-climax, conflict
Three of Wands	*Upright*: beginnings, optimism, luck *Reversed*: delay, indecision, procrastination
Four of Wands	*Upright*: creativity, openness, adventure *Reversed*: frustration, resentment
Five of Wands	*Upright*: challenge, growth, satisfaction *Reversed*: setbacks, conflict, argument
Six of Wands	*Upright*: good fortune, reward, satisfaction *Reversed*: delay, misunderstanding
Seven of Wands	*Upright*: effort, success, fulfilment *Reversed*: failure, self-doubt
Eight of Wands	*Upright*: progress, completion, fulfilment *Reversed*: confusion, misdirection

Nine of Wands	*Upright*: resilience, reward *Reversed*: reluctance, failure, conflict
Ten of Wands	*Upright*: responsibility, commitment *Reversed*: exhaustion, confusion
Page of Wands	*Upright*: energy, vigour, new beginnings *Reversed*: apathy, mistrust, suspicion
Knight of Wands	*Upright*: excitement, unpredictability *Reversed*: stress, impatience, recklessness
Queen of Wands	*Upright*: energy, ability, purpose *Reversed*: interference, arrogance
King of Wands	*Upright*: intelligence, generosity *Reversed*: intolerence, narrow-mindedness

Cups

Ace of Cups	*Upright*: love, emotion, growth *Reversed*: sadness, loneliness, disappointment
Two of Cups	*Upright*: support, trust, friendship *Reversed*: conflict, betrayal, separation
Three of Cups	*Upright*: optimism, growth *Reversed*: selfishness, exploitation
Four of Cups	*Upright*: boredom, apathy *Reversed*: self-pity, indulgence
Five of Cups	*Upright*: unhappiness, regret, loss *Reversed*: remorse, sadness
Six of Cups	*Upright*: reminiscing, rewards *Reversed*: nostalgia, delay
Seven of Cups	*Upright*: illusion, choice *Reversed*: delusion, fantasy
Eight of Cups	*Upright*: development, sacrifice, growth *Reversed*: uncertainty, change
Nine of Cups	*Upright*: happiness, optimism, generosity *Reversed*: complacency, superficiality
Ten of Cups	*Upright*: fulfilment, contentment *Reversed*: disruption, unhappiness

Page of Cups	*Upright*: sensitivity, modesty *Reversed*: dissatisfaction, apathy
Knight of Cups	*Upright*: idealism, originality, optimism *Reversed*: deception, concealment
Queen of Cups	*Upright*: sensitivity, kindness *Reversed*: vanity, selfishness
King of Cups	*Upright*: sophistication, coldness *Reversed*: deception, manipulation

Swords

Ace of Swords	*Upright*: intellect, reason, fairness *Reversed*: injustice, bias, frustration
Two of Swords	*Upright*: argument, breakdown *Reversed*: conflict, aggression
Three of Swords	*Upright*: conflict, change *Reversed*: suffering, frustration
Four of Swords	*Upright*: recovery, renewal *Reversed*: isolation, loneliness
Five of Swords	*Upright*: humiliation, defeat *Reversed*: dishonesty, trickery
Six of Swords	*Upright*: renewal, rebirth *Reversed*: delay, postponement
Seven of Swords	*Upright*: intelligence, unorthodoxy *Reversed*: timidity, conservatism, fear
Eight of Swords	*Upright*: delay, obstruction *Reversed*: helplessness, frustration
Nine of Swords	*Upright*: anxiety, worry, suspicion *Reversed*: depression, isolation
Ten of Swords	*Upright*: caution, progress *Reversed*: conflict, difficulty
Page of Swords	*Upright*: caution, tact, wariness *Reversed*: mistrust, suspicion
Knight of Swords	*Upright*: courage, conviction, strength *Reversed*: aggression, impatience

Queen of Swords	*Upright*: independence, ambition
	Reversed: loneliness, coldness
King of Swords	*Upright*: authority, power, innovation
	Reversed: cruelty, exploitation

Pentacles

Ace of Pentacles	*Upright*: stability, security, contentment
	Reversed: instability, anxiety
Two of Pentacles	*Upright*: contentment, optimism
	Reversed: impatience, recklessness
Three of Pentacles	*Upright*: reward, satisfaction
	Reversed: frustration, criticism
Four of Pentacles	*Upright*: security, predictability
	Reversed: reluctance, resistance
Five of Pentacles	*Upright*: difficulty, insecurity
	Reversed: isolation, helplessness
Six of Pentacles	*Upright*: fairness, generosity
	Reversed: unhappiness, carelessness
Seven of Pentacles	*Upright*: perseverence, effort, luck
	Reversed: defeat, acceptance
Eight of Pentacles	*Upright*: progress, prosperity, pride
	Reversed: frustration, worry
Nine of Pentacles	*Upright*: achievement, security, solitude
	Reversed: insecurity, dependency
Ten of Pentacles	*Upright*: security, support
	Reversed: interference, hindrance
Page of Pentacles	*Upright*: dependability, security
	Reversed: frustration, unhappiness
Knight of Pentacles	*Upright*: practicality, dependability
	Reversed: stagnation, boredom
Queen of Pentacles	*Upright*: openness, sensitivity, generosity
	Reversed: materialism, insecurity
King of Pentacles	*Upright*: honesty, practicality, security
	Reversed: greed, weakness